CAIRNS
AND SURROUNDS

Cairns, gateway to Tropical North Queensland, basks in glorious sunshine. It is a city of great charm and character: its buildings reflect both its history and its up-to-the-minute modernity. Its people are warm and welcoming. The Cairns International Airport and the city's abundance of accommodation bring the world to this region of natural wonders.

Situated in the centre of some of the most scenic and ecologically important areas in the world, Cairns is the stepping-stone to a natural treasure-trove of plains, tableland, rainforest and reef. The city itself has many attractions – international cuisine, great shopping, cinemas, theatres, museums and botanical gardens, all set among the cool greens and brilliant colours of tropical vegetation.

Travelling north, south, east or west from Cairns, there is much to see and do. There is the blissful relaxation of lazing on glistening white beaches under azure skies; the sheer pleasure of sailing among coral cays set like jewels in sparkling seas; the adrenaline rush of whitewater rafting; the visual feast of the World-Heritage-listed Great Barrier Reef (one of the greatest natural wonders on Earth); the cathedral-like atmosphere of some of the oldest and most important rainforest in the world; the triumph of landing a majestic Black Marlin; the heart stopping excitement of coming face-to-face with a Southern Cassowary, an Amethystine Python, or, from a respectable distance, an Estuarine Crocodile. Tropical North Queensland has it all.

PASCAL
PRESS

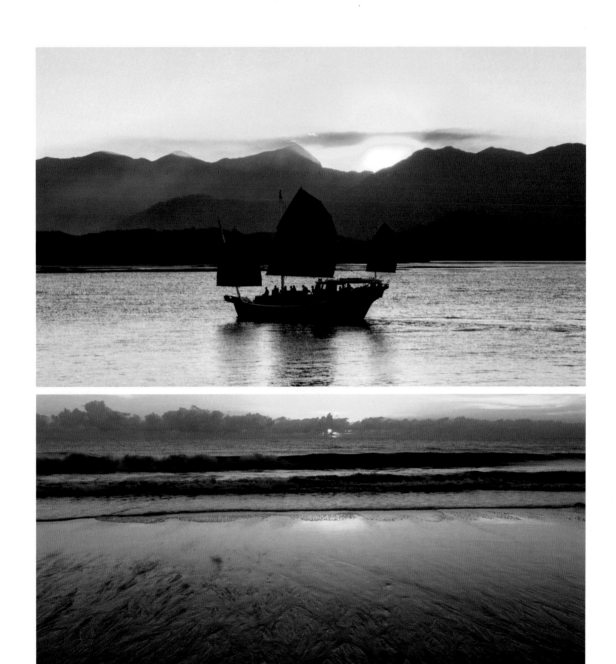

THE MAGIC OF THE TROPICS

"The Tropics" conjures up images of sparkling clear waters, brilliantly coloured coral reefs and fish, and lush rainforest. In Tropical North Queensland all these promises are kept. Today we are aware that, as well as providing adventure, the reefs and rainforests are among the most beautiful and fragile environments on Earth. If the bounteous natural gifts of the region are treated with caution and respect, the visitor will be richly rewarded with unforgettable experiences of excitement and breathtaking beauty.

Above and opposite: Sunrise and sunset turn the tropical sea to liquid fire as enjoy its beauty.

CAIRNS

Cairns is the tourist capital of north Queensland. It is the jumping-off point for reef, rainforest, beaches, tableland and the outback. But it is much more than that—Cairns is the centre of diverse economic activity, including farming of sugar cane and tropical produce of all kinds. Tourism and industry mix harmoniously with the natural environment.

Cairns, like many other northern towns and cities, began as a port from which to ship timber, beef, gold and minerals from the inland. It lies in Trinity Bay, near the mouth of the Barron River. The population is a glorious mix of races and nationalities, from the original Djabuganydji people and the descendants of South Sea Islanders who were brought to work on the sugar fields, to post-war European immigrants.

Today, Cairns is an exciting city, a gateway for international travellers, and it has world-class facilities, including a casino, restaurants, botanic gardens, shops, theatres and galleries to be enjoyed in tropical sunshine under clear blue skies.

Left: Looking over the lush surroundings of the Reef Hotel Casino with the city beyond.

Above: The Lagoon, seen from above, provides a cool change on a sultry summer day.

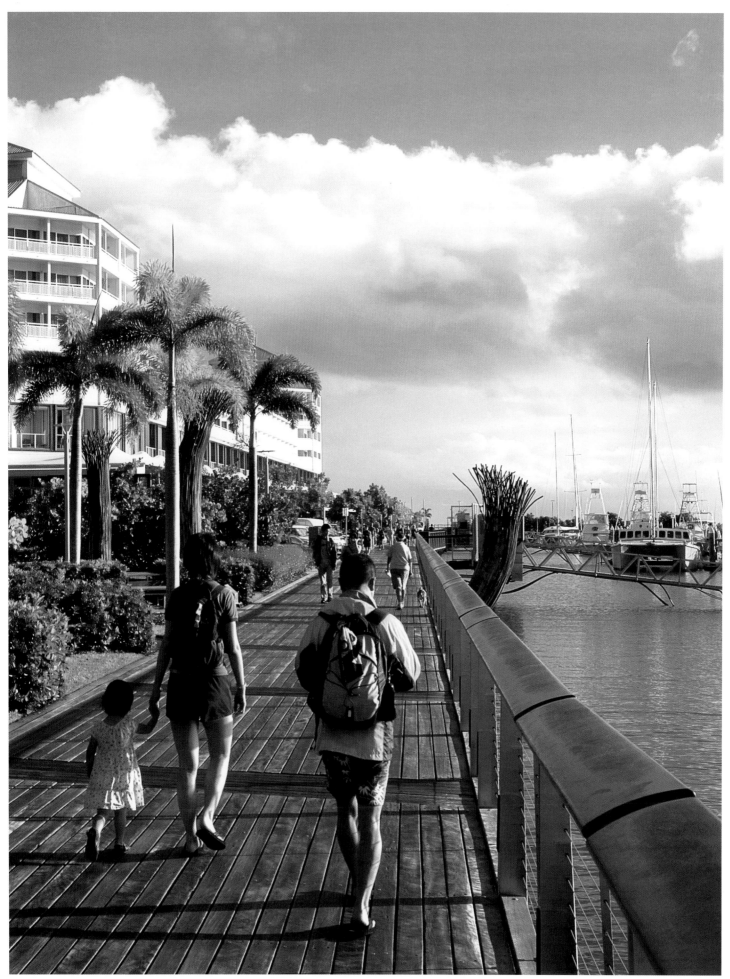

Above: Visitors can enjoy a relaxing stroll on the walkway heading towards the Pier Marketplace.

LAZY DAYS

The Esplanade is central to the spirit of Cairns—it is a meeting place, but also a place where anyone can find solitude and relax in the sun. At low tide, birds hunt on the mudflats and dreamers on the shore watch them while joggers exercise, families stroll and holiday-makers catch their breath after a day on the reef. Just to the north lie sandy beaches fringed with palms, and everywhere the glistening peacock blues and greens of the sea cool the eye.

Above: Despite the area's popularity, there is plenty of room to stretch out in the sun.
Opposite top: Quiet, sandy beaches lie north of Cairns. *Opposite bottom:* Take a stroll along the beach at Palm Cove.

A THRIVING CITY

Cairns began as a sleepy port for shipping gold, tin and timber from the Atherton Tableland and the Hodgkinson River goldfield, and was even in danger of being overtaken by Smithfield, 12 kilometres to the north, or Port Douglas, yet further north. It has since grown to become a thriving modern city.

Cairns has a busy social calendar, including September's annual Festival Cairns, a celebration of tropical Australia's diverse cultural life. The Cairns Museum preserves local European and Indigenous history, while the Freshwater Connection is a railway museum. The city also has a lively theatre and entertainment scene.

Cairns is a particularly wonderful placc to shop — the Pier Marketplace, the City Place Mall, weekend markets, art galleries, bookshops, music shops, crafts, clothes and jewellery produced by local designers, Aboriginal art and artefacts ... there is so much to see and still more to buy.

Above: Cairns Convention Centre. *Left:* A view over Cairns Harbour, the Foreshore Promenade, and Trinity Inlet. *Inset, from left:* City Place; children enjoy a close encounter during the Reef & Rainforest Carnivale; historic Hides Corner; Reef Hotel Casino viewed through Esplanade palms.

WHEN THE SUN
GOES DOWN

Soft, velvet tropical nights follow hot, sunny days. Gaming is popular at the casino, as well as spectacular live shows, restaurants and bars. In the city centre are nightclubs and live music venues. Restaurants of every type and cuisine are scattered throughout the city and suburbs, offering the opportunity to eat quickly before sampling the night-life, or dine leisurely while gazing at the water, the mountains or the lights.

Top: Cairns sparkles at night. Cape Grafton looms in the background across Trinity Inlet. *Opposite:* Along the Esplanade at night. *Right:* The cool glow of twilight replaces the glare of a clear day.

FUN AFTER DARK

The restaurants of Cairns offer all styles of food—from modern Australian prepared by brilliant young chefs to classical Asian and European cuisines. Dining out in a city where so much heavenly food comes from the sea and where tropical fruits and vegetables thrive in the rich volcanic soil is bound to be a joy. The casino sparkles, inviting people to stop by, but it is just one of Cairns's night spots. Nightclubs and hotels welcome visitors for a meal, a drink, dancing or live music of most varieties. Cinemas and the Cairns Civic Theatre offer still more choices.

Opposite top: The view to Cairns Harbour, at dusk. *Bottom:* Dining alfresco on a balmy tropical night. *Above:* The Reef Hotel Casino, lit up for another night of entertainment.

Top: Aboriginal art on display in one of the art shops.

Bottom: Budget accommodation and dining line the streets of Cairns.

Above: The Lagoon, on the Cairns Foreshore, is an inviting and safe place for a swim.

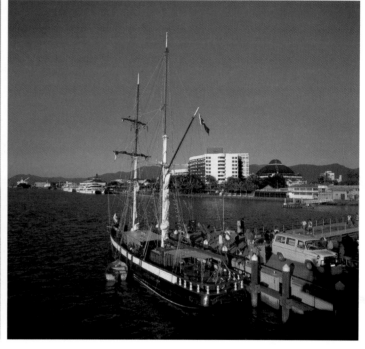

OUT TO THE CORAL SEA

Escaping to the reefs, islands and cays across the clear blue water of the Coral Sea is a wonderful experience. Boats of all kinds are your passport to this magical World Heritage Area. The beauty and diversity of the Great Barrier Reef has to be seen to be believed. A natural wonder of the world, the Reef is a complex structure made up of many reefs, and it is home to about 1500 species of fish and about 400 types of coral.

Top: Boats are safely moored in Marlin Marina. *Bottom left:* A junk-rigged boat adds a touch of the exotic to the scene. *Bottom right:* History sits elegantly afloat—a square-rigger lies at its mooring. *Opposite:* Bare-boating or chartering allow exploration at your own pace, with the added fun of sailing.

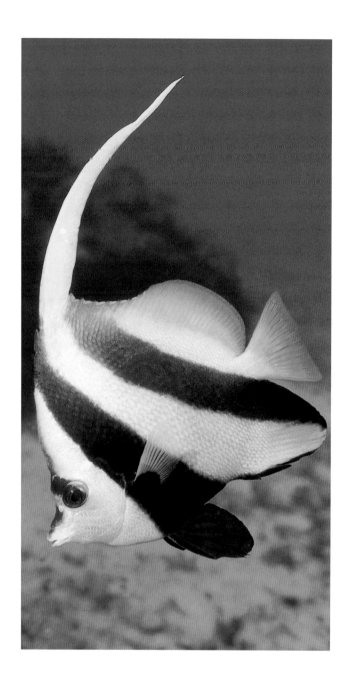

A DAY ON GREEN ISLAND

Green Island is the closest island to Cairns. A classically teardrop-shaped coral cay, it lies north-east of Trinity Bay. Many day trips go to Green Island from Cairns, allowing visitors to view the reef from the underwater observatory, take trips in glass-bottom boats, and snorkel. It is an easy walk around the 12 hectare island to see the plant and bird life. Green Island also boasts a low-rise resort, and visits to Marineland Melanesia.

Left: Green Island's jetty stretches out to receive visitors.
Inset: Snorkelling in reef waters can open up a whole new world, such as seeing an anemonefish (centre) which lives unharmed in the stinging tentacles of a sea anemone.
Above: Bannerfish cruise close to the protecting reef—their home, shelter and source of food.

21

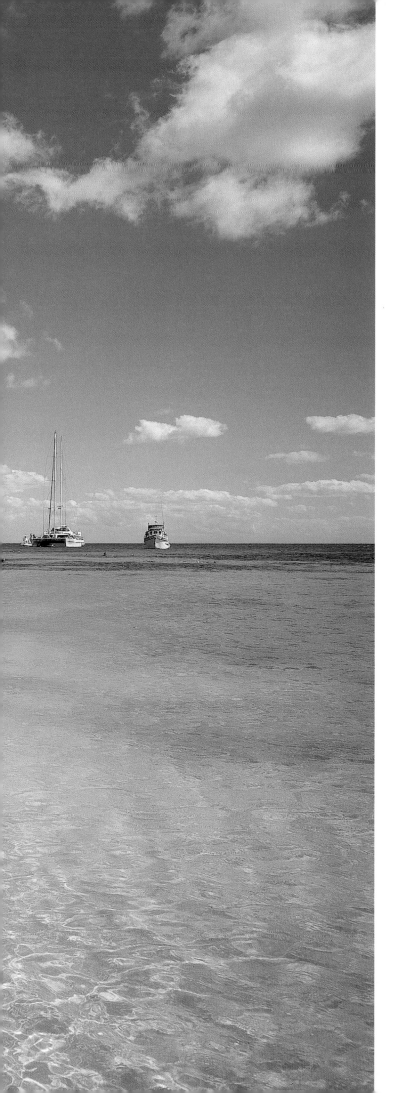

SAFARI TO MICHAELMAS CAY

North by north-east from Green Island is Michaelmas Cay and Michaelmas Reef, just over 50 kilometres from Cairns. Here the broad sweep of sea, sand and sky banish the cares of the workaday world.

Scuba diving and snorkelling on the reef are two of the main pastimes, but taking a reef walk at low tide is an absolute delight. Crabs, anemones and all manner of tiny sea creatures live dual lives—under water and above water. Tour guides advise on where to go, what to beware of and how to avoid damaging this fragile water garden. Michaelmas Cay is also an important breeding site for seabirds, such as Sooty Terns and Common Noddies.

Left: Surely nowhere on Earth has dancing water of such clarity as on the Reef. *Below:* Awed scuba divers drift near coral formations.

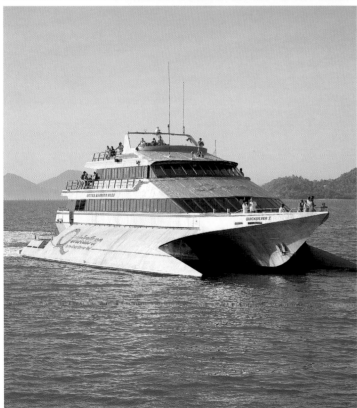

THE OUTER BARRIER REEF

Trips to the outer reef can last a day, or a week or more. The choice is yours, governed only by time and budget. This is serious diving territory—it really does not get any better. Hastings, Moore, Norman and Ribbon Reefs, the Cod Hole, Flinders Reef: the names have magic. Nonetheless, this whole area is very much more than a tourist playground. The Great Barrier Reef Marine Park is a large laboratory and research facility which aims to preserve and protect the reef and gain understanding of such creatures as the Crown of Thorns sea star which appear to be a threat.

Top left: Having some fun in the sun. *Top right:* Snorkelling is great, and you need little practice before you can really start exploring. *Bottom left:* The speedy tourist catamarans make nothing of distance. *Opposite:* Boats dot the reef surrounds while a large cruise boat is moored at the reef station.

BARRON GORGE

The Barron River tumbles down the Barron Gorge on its way from the Atherton Tableland to the coast. A trip on the Kuranda Scenic Railway, one of the greatest short railway journeys in the world, gives a spectacular view of the Falls and the Gorge. This is often the first glimpse of the northern rainforests that visitors can witness, and it gives an overview of the splendour of the forests and an idea of the massive geological time that went into creation of the landscape.

Left: The Kuranda railway station and its beautiful gardens are the perfect introduction to the Atherton Tableland.
Above: The magnificent Barron Falls at their awe-inspiring best.
Opposite: The Scenic Railway passes Stoney Creek Falls.

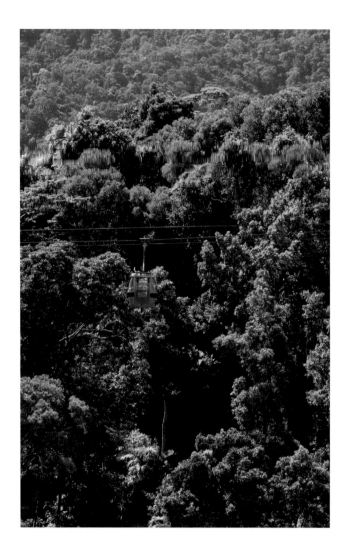

SKYRAIL THROUGH THE RAINFOREST

The Skyrail trip is the longest cable car journey in the world, swooping above the treetops for 7.5 kilometres between Smithfield and Kuranda. Many visitors to Kuranda travel one way by the railway and the other by the Skyrail. The cable car makes two stops on its way—once where travellers can walk to look out at the Barron Falls, and once at a rainforest interpretative centre. From the Skyrail, vistas of the coast and the tableland arc spread out all round, as well as views of the forest canopy at close quarters.

Above: Soaring above the treetops. *Left:* The Skyrail provides magnificent views of the Barron River.

KURANDA — VILLAGE IN THE RAINFOREST

Ever since the railway opened in 1891, sightseers have travelled from Cairns to Kuranda, a village steeped in history as well as being situated in an area of immense botanical and zoological significance. This peaceful, laid-back town begins to hum with activity on market days and the Rainforestation Nature Park, a 40-hectare tourist attraction set amongst World Heritage rainforest, is only a five minutes drive from Kuranda Village.

Above left: A Southern Cassowary, just one of the many species found at Rainforestation Nature Park. *Right:* The Kuranda markets, where visitors can buy all manner of craft goods.

ABORIGINAL THEATRE

Smithfield is the home of the Tjapukai Dance Theatre, an internationally renowned local Aboriginal dance troupe. The performances explain a little of the Indigenous culture as well as displaying the performers' dance skills. The Tjapukai Aboriginal Cultural Park has seven seperate arenas showcasing all aspects of Aboriginal culture, including art galleries and interactive areas for visitors to learn boomerang throwing and didgeridoo playing.

Visitors can take the Dreamtime Walk and see the Pamagirri Aboriginal Dancers perform at the Rainforestation Nature Park — all of these artists are working to keep traditional tales alive, as well as creating contemporary dances to describe modern tribal life and experiences.

Above and left: Members of the Tjapukai Dance Theatre take delight in performing traditional and modern Aboriginal dances in full costume for visitors.

ENTER THE MAGIC
RAINFOREST

Nothing can prepare the newcomer for the majesty of the wet tropics rainforests of north Queensland, and words simply cannot describe the awe visitors feel. Around the township of Kuranda are many walks through the forest and the residents have developed several parks and enclosed walks that help visitors view the less visible flora and fauna; for instance, the wildlife noctarium, where nocturnal animals such as gliders, larger possums, fruit bats and echidnas can be seen. The butterfly sanctuary is equally delightful. Sightseers can paddle canoes along the Barron River to experience the forest from the water.

Top: Guided tours of the aviaries are held at the Australian Butterfly Sanctuary, Kuranda.
Bottom left: A male Dainty Green Tree Frog calls for a mate.
Bottom right: A Green Ringtail Possum. *Opposite:* The quiet beauty of the rainforest is an ideal antidote for the stress of the workaday world.

EXPLORING THE TABLELAND

The Atherton Tableland offers an equally beautiful but quieter life than the coastal region. Here are many farms, crater lakes such as Lakes Barrine and Eacham, Tinaroo Dam, national parks and wildlife reserves. To the west of the Tableland are historical mining towns like Herberton, the site of the original tin mines, and Chillagoe where copper, tin and silver-lead has been mined, and where gold and marble are still mined.

Top left: The lush pasture of the Tableland. *Bottom left:* The Grand Hotel, Atherton, another historic hotel. *Right:* Tourists inspect a Curtain Fig at Yungaburra. *Opposite:* Water cruises on Lake Barrine, a delightful way to see the spectacular vegetation and wildlife.

THE WORLD OF WATERFALLS

All of the rivers that rush from the Tableland to the narrow coastal plain freefall in places and tumble down boisterous rapids in other spots—the Tully, the Johnston, the Russell, the Mulgrave, the Barron, Mossman Gorge, the Daintree. The rainfall in the north is high, and even higher on the Tableland, much of which is some 900 metres above sea-level.

Left: The beautiful Nandroya Falls, Wooroonooran National Park. *Below:* Tchupala Falls, Wooroonooran National Park. *Opposite (clockwise from top left):* Ellinjaa Falls, Atherton Tableland; Millstream Falls, Atherton Tableland; Josephine Falls, Wooroonooran National Park. *Following pages:* Millaa Millaa Falls, Atherton Tableland.

WILD WATER

Wherever the rivers of the north break into rapids, free spirits can be found rafting the whitewater. For the ultimate experience of the thrill of pitting human skills, strength and endurance against the power of nature, there is little to match whitewater rafting, and the rivers of the wet tropics of north Queensland provide ideal conditions for this exciting sport.

Left and above: Whitewater rafting on the Tully River.

41

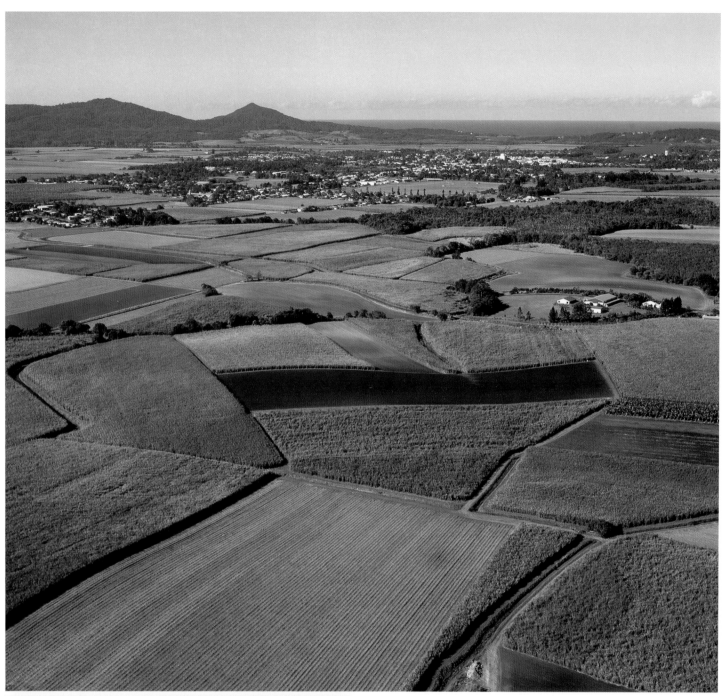

CANE FARMING

Sugarcane has been the faithful staple of the tropic north's economy. When the goldrushes of the late nineteenth and early twentieth centuries died away, most of the population grew to rely on the sugar industry for their livelihood. Towns were established to service canefarmers' needs and people worked growing, cutting and milling cane, and then refining the sugar and making the many sugar byproducts.

Above: The canefields extend up into the hills behind the city of Cairns. Seen from the air, they form a magnificent countryside patchwork. *Left:* Harvesting the cane.

NORTH FROM CAIRNS

As travellers wend their way up the coast on the Cook Highway from Cairns, they will be treated to views of some of the most beautiful coastline in Australia. In many places it looks as if the mountains are tumbling into the clear water of the Coral Sea. Apart from Port Douglas, this is where the least heavily populated section of the Queensland coast begins.

Right: The Cook Highway snakes along the coastline south of Port Douglas. *Below:* The Bouncing Stones are an unusual geological formation along this stretch of coastline. *Following pages:* Palm Cove, paradise on Earth!

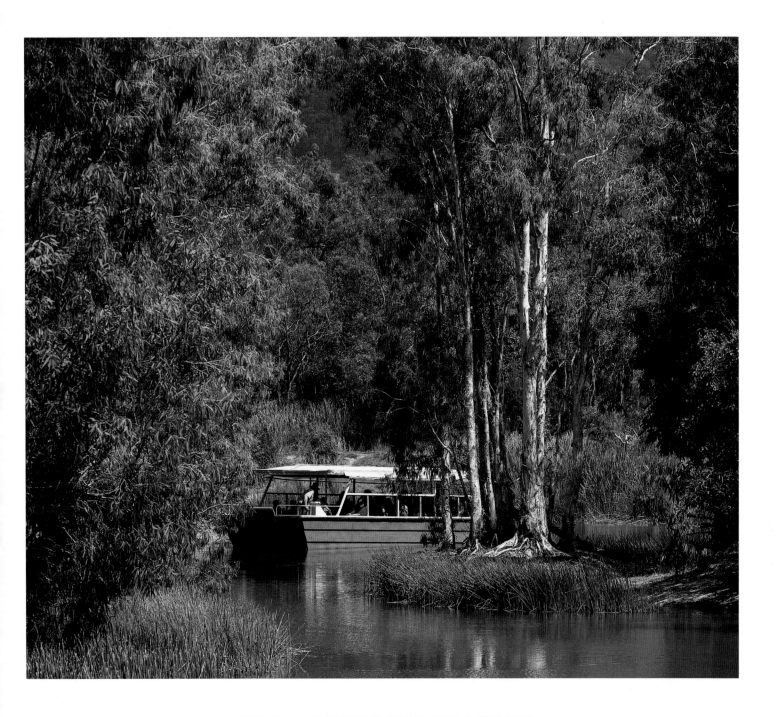

THE NORTHERN BEACHES

The beaches north of Cairns—Machans Beach, Holloways Beach, Yorkeys Knob, Trinity Beach, Clifton Beach, Palm Cove and Ellis Beach—are known as the Marlin Coast. They make pleasant stopping points on a leisurely trip to Port Douglas and points further north. Wide stretches of sand line much of the shore, and palms fringe these golden lips on the calm water. From Palm Cove it is only a few hundred metres to Double Island, a beautiful little island on which there is a luxury resort that can be reached by water taxi. Those travelling along the scenic coastal road can also stop off and enjoy the exciting and educational wildlife presentations at Hartley's Crocodile Adventures.

Opposite: Ellis Beach, where the mountains meet the sea. *Above:* Visitors relax on an eco tour of Hartley's Lagoon at Hartley's Crocodile Adventures.

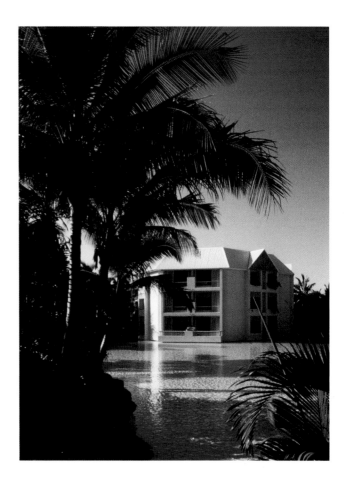

PORT DOUGLAS

Port Douglas is the glamour capital of the north, now famous throughout the world as the place where even the US President can holiday safely and privately. Port Douglas was founded in 1877 as a port for the Hodgkinson River goldfield, and was named after John Douglas, a former premier of Queensland. It first hit the news in a big way with the building of the Sheraton Mirage, which was followed by the Radisson Royal Palms resort and a championship golf course.

However, Port Douglas has kept its relaxed charm and has plenty of accommodation for backpackers and families. It is an excellent point for trips to the Low Isles, the Mossman Gorge, the Daintree, Cape Tribulation and the Reef, or Cape York and the Gulf. Just 6 kilometres from the heart of Port Douglas, the Rainforest Habitat Wildlife Sanctuary lets visitors stroll through unique environments that depict over 180 species of the surrounding rainforest, wetlands, woodlands and grasslands.

Above: Luxury resorts are nestled into magnificent surrounds. *Left:* Yachts berthed at Marina Mirage. *Inset, from left:* The Courthouse Hotel; Marina Mirage shopping centre; a fern fringed walkway; male Eclectus Parrot, Rainforest Habitat.

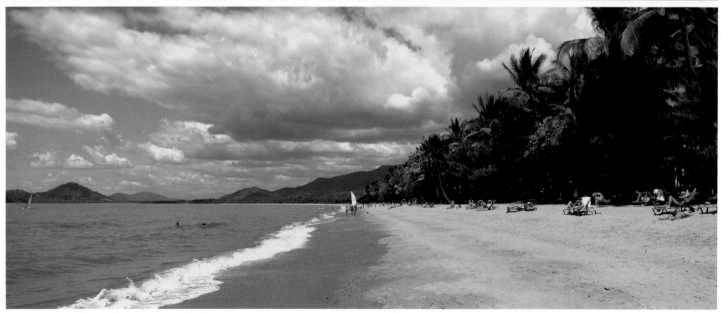

Above: Four Mile Beach at Port Douglas has something for everyone — spectacular scenery or just lazing in the sun.
Opposite: The sheltered waters surrounding Port Douglas provide a picture-perfect start and finish for sailing in the tropical north.

A DAY AT LOW ISLE

A lighthouse dating from 1878 stands on this coral cay sitting within a surrounding lagoon where visitors have a chance to explore the magnificence of the Great Barrier Reef at close quarters. Sailboats, catamarans and large and small power boats all make their way to the Low Isles, where holiday-makers go snorkelling and diving, take trips in a glass-bottom boat, swim, or go for a guided walk with a marine biologist.

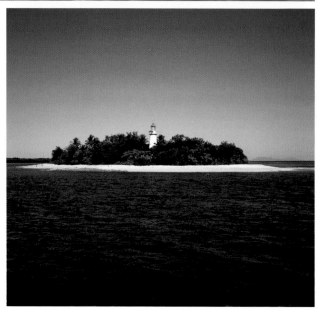

Top: Low tide gives visitors a chance to study the reef's many different forms of life. *Bottom:* An idyllic day on the beach. *Right:* The lighthouse rises from its surrounding vegetation. *Opposite: Wavedancer III*, with daytrippers aboard, edges toward anchorage.

MOSSMAN GORGE

Just 5 kilometres west of the town of Mossman, in the south of the World Heritage-listed Daintree National Park, lies the Mossman Gorge. It is impossible to look at the Gorge and not feel the awe that the first Europeans must have experienced when they stumbled on its primeval beauty. The water is always cool because it is shaded by the forest, and lichens, moss and ferns thrive on the rocks and in the crevices between them. Walking trails lead off from the carpark and, beyond the swimming holes, a suspension bridge carries walkers to a 2.5 kilometre circuit through the rainforest.

Fifty million years ago, almost all of Australia was covered in rainforest but, because of climate changes, nearly all of it had gone by the time the Aborigines arrived in Australia. Today, only about 20 000 square kilometres of rainforest is left, more than half in Queensland. The tropical rainforest has a special place in Australians' hearts, living as they do in a largely dry continent. Research continues so that we can enjoy and preserve the forests.

Above: The White-lipped Tree Frog may be spotted by vigilant hikers. *Right:* The wild Mossman River tumbles through the Gorge on its way to the sea.

DAINTREE RAINFOREST

Daintree, originally a logging town, lies east of the Daintree National Park, where some of the oldest forests in the world can be found. Bushwalking in the park is an unforgettable experience. The Daintree is one of the richest storehouses of plants and animals in the world, many species being found nowhere else, and scientists and nature lovers flock here to study and observe. The Daintree Rainforest Environmental Centre has been set up for visitors to learn more about the forest as they walk along self-guided boardwalks or watch films about the forest in the centre's theatre.

The Amethystine Python (*top*) and the Herbert River Ringtail Possum (*bottom*) are some familiar inhabitants of the Daintree. *Left:* The Daintree impresses visitors with its lush vegetation and its cathedral-like quietness.

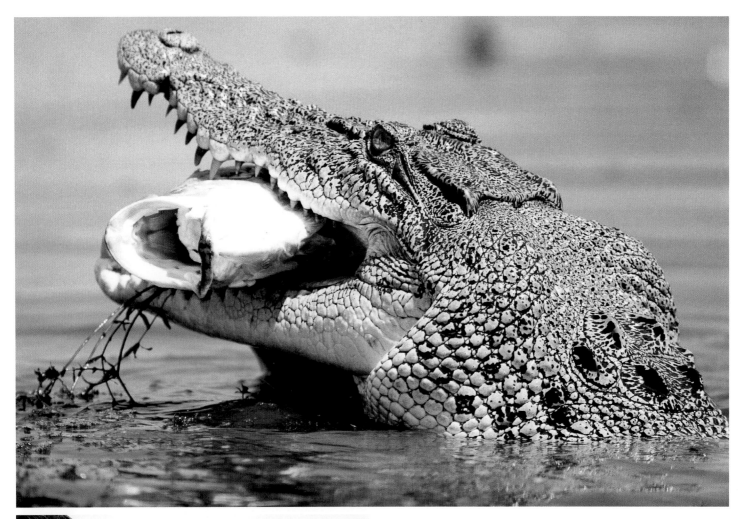

DAINTREE RIVER

The Daintree is crocodile territory, and that means the dangerous Estuarine Crocodiles as well as the harmless freshwater species. These prehistoric saurians inhabit mangroves, coastal creeks and estuaries. Plenty of the Estuarine breed can be seen in safety at the various crocodile farms and crocodile parks throughout the Tropical North.

Boat trips along the Daintree are an excellent way to see more of the forest and observe the local plant and wildlife. A boat trip is a blissfully relaxing alternative to walking the rainforest trails. The Alexandra Range Lookout offers panoramic views of the Daintree River's estuary and the national park.

Top: Dinner time for a Daintree salty. *Above left:* The "Big Barramundi" tourist centre. *Left:* Exploring by boat. *Opposite (clockwise from top):* The estuary of the Daintree; Ulysses Butterfly; male Cairns Birdwing Butterfly; Cooktown orchids, Queensland's floral symbol.

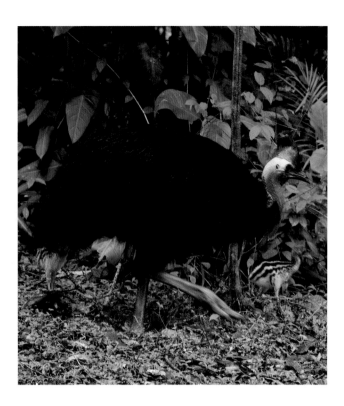

A VISIT TO CASSOWARY COUNTRY

In a forest of fan palms north of the Daintree River one of the two remaining cassowary colonies in Queensland can be found. (The other small colony is near Mission Beach, south of Cairns.) The cassowary is a large flightless bird, not as tall as the emu, but more heavily built. These birds are crucial in the forest because they are the only dispersal agents for some 70 plant species and the main dispersal agents for at least 30 more. This means that these seeds are spread by the cassowaries, which eat the fruit and then deposit the seeds in their droppings on the forest floor. Scientists have estimated the entire population of Australian cassowaries at 1500 adult birds. Their reduction in numbers is due to destruction of habitat and careless driving. Feral animals, such as dogs and pigs, also pose a significant threat. These animals are very partial to cassowary egg for supper and they will kill young or ailing birds.

Above and top: The endangered Southern Cassowary occupies tropical rainforest habitat in north-eastern Queensland. *Right:* The World Heritage habitat that typifies the Daintree is also where this magnificient flightless bird calls home.

A DAY AT CAPE TRIBULATION

Captain Cook named Cape Tribulation on one of his trips along Queensland's coast when he feared he may never get away from the reefs and back into deep water. The region's unique value and beauty was acknowledged when the Cape Tribulation National Park, spreading from the Daintree to the Bloomfield River, was declared in 1981.

Top left: A palm-fringed beach near the Cape. *Top right:* Cape Tribulation from afar. *Bottom left:* Exploring the mangroves at low-tide. *Bottom right:* Trunk of the Bumpy Satin Ash. *Opposite (clockwise from top left):* Part of the coastline seen from the road; mangroves on the shore—provide valuable habitat for fish; an aerial shot of the Cape in all its splendour.

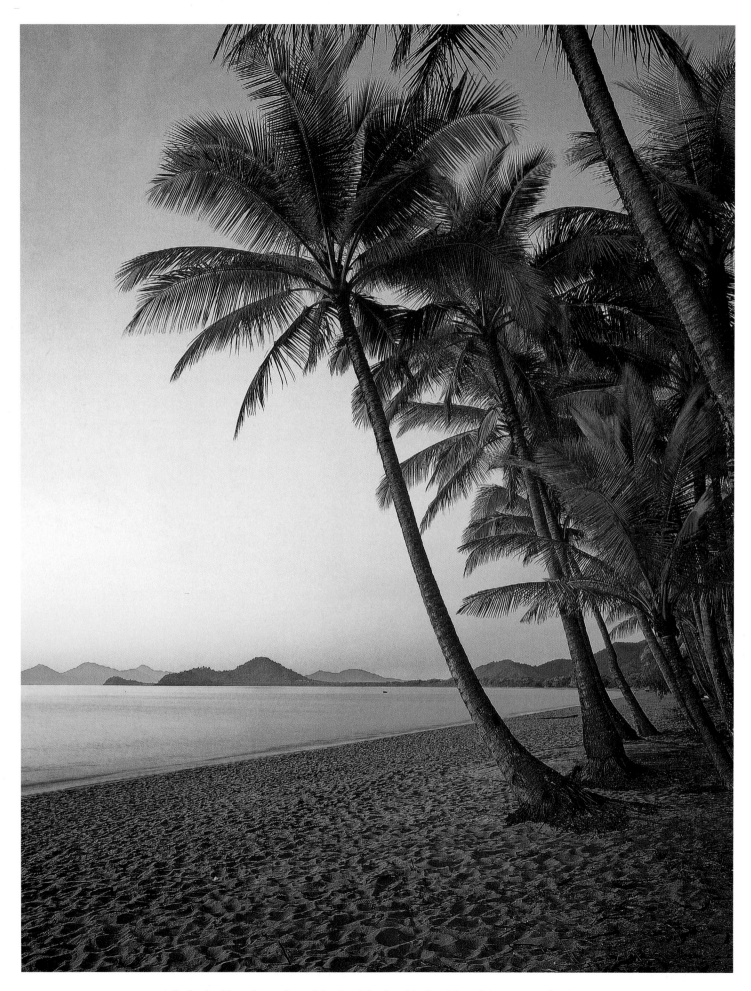

A flash of gold on the surface of the Coral Sea heralds the rising of the sun at Palm Cove.